This Book Belongs To:

Wayfinders LITTLE BIOGRAPHIES OF HAWAI'I'S LEADERS

MARY KAWENA PUKUI

KNOWLEDGE IS LIFE

written by David Del Rocco
illustrated by Storm Kano

BeachHouse

Mary Abigail Tui Kawena'ulaokalaniohi'iakaikapoli-opelekawahine'aihonua Wiggin (we will call her Kawena) was born on April 20, 1895, in the hot, dry Ka'ū district of Hawai'i island. She was a child of two worlds.

Her father was a Caucasian man from Salem, Massachusetts, and her mother was Native Hawaiian, descended from kāhuna, or priests, of Pele, Hawai'i's goddess of fire and volcanoes. Kawena was raised speaking both English and Hawaiian.

Her name "Kawena" means
the rosy glow of the sky at sunrise.

She was born during a time of turmoil in the islands.

Two years before her birth, the Hawaiian monarchy was overthrown and a new government began to rule.

In 1896, when Kawena was just a year old, this new government outlawed the Hawaiian language. It could no longer be used in schools. In 1898, when Kawena was three years old, Hawai'i lost its independence and became a territory of the United States.

In an old Hawaiian tradition called hānai, Kawena was given in adoption to her grandmother. She lived with her in Nāʻālehu near her parents' house until her grandmother passed away when Kawena was six. Kawena strongly believed in aloha ʻāina, which means "love of the land" and so much more.

Hawaiians have a very deep connection to the land. Kawena was brought up to love her Hawaiian culture, particularly the language and the hula. Her grandmother was a court dancer for Queen Emma.

Kawena later became a kumu hula and taught hula for many years.

One of the most memorable events in her childhood happened when her great-grandmother passed away. The whole family took a journey at midnight to the volcano crater. The bones of her great-grandmother were cleaned and wrapped in kapa (cloth made of tree bark). The bundle was then tossed into the burning crater while the family prayed and chanted.

When she was a child, Kawena had a pet goat named Nancy. It did not like boys and would butt any boys that came near Kawena!

In the early 1900s, Kawena and her parents moved to Honolulu on the island of O‘ahu, where she attended a missionary school: Kawaiaha‘o Seminary for Girls.

One day, a new student showed up at school who spoke very little English. Kawena helped her by speaking to her in Hawaiian. A teacher overheard and scolded Kawena for speaking Hawaiian.

As her punishment, for one week she had to eat only bread and water for lunch in front of the other students. Kawena's mother was so angry when she heard about this, she decided Kawena would never return. So at the age of fifteen, Kawena left school.

Kawena was a brilliant woman who often said, "Knowledge, to me, is life." At age fifteen, she began collecting traditional Hawaiian sayings called ʻōlelo noʻeau. This was a lifelong work that eventually became one of her most famous books.

In 1913, Kawena married Napoleon Kaloli'i Pukui. Because they had no children and Kawena very much wanted children, they adopted a baby girl who they named Patience (Pat for short) and then a second girl named Faith.

When Kawena was twenty-three, she attended the Seventh Day Adventist Hawaiian Mission Academy, and at age twenty-eight, she received her high school diploma.

Many years later, Kawena gave birth to a third daughter, who they named Pelehonuamea.

E ka iwa
KA IWA
MARY K. PUKUI

In 1937, she began to work at the Bishop Museum. In addition to all the books she wrote and translated while working there, she composed over 150 songs and chants. She also interviewed many kūpuna, recording their stories and their traditions.

As a natural teacher and storyteller, Kawena passed on her knowledge of the Hawaiian language and culture to her three daughters. She also taught at Punahou School for many years and later at Kamehameha Schools. Punahou School has honored her by naming its new learning commons after her.

Kawena passed away at the age of ninety-one in 1986.

Nobody has done more for the Hawaiian language and culture than Mary Kawena Pukui. She wrote more than fifty books about the Hawaiian language, culture, and ʻike Hawaiʻi (Hawaiian knowledge), inspiring Hawaiʻi's future by preserving its past.

LIST OF SOURCES

Keepers of the Flame: The Cultural Legacy of Three Hawaiian Women (film). The Hawaiian Legacy Foundation, Honolulu, HI, 2005.

"Kūkahekahe: Celebrating Mary Kawena Pukui." Kamehameha Schools, Honolulu, HI. April 20, 2022.

"Life Story: Mary Kawena Pukui (1895–1986)." Women and the American Story, New York Historical Society Museum & Library.
https://wams.nyhistory.org/confidence-and-crises/great-depression/mary-kawena-pukui/

"Mary Kawena Pukui." Hawai'i Council for the Humanities. Honolulu, HI, 2021.
https://hihumanities.org/what-we-do/hi-history-day/hawai%CA%BBi-history-day-honorees/mary-kawena-pukui/

Mary Kawena Pukui (film) "PBS Hawai'i Presents: Classics #202." Honolulu, HI. May 9, 1984.

Mary Kawena Pukui Preservation Society
https://marykawenapukui.com/bio1-10/

Trust for Public Land, December 24, 2020
https://www.tpl.org/blog/grandson-follows-ancient-footsteps-help-save-his-family-ancestral-home

Author's note: Although Pūku'i is the spelling of her last name with modern-day diacritics, during her lifetime, Mary Kawena Pukui chose to spell it without the diacritics as her husband did.

About the Author

David Del Rocco is a high school teacher who lives and works in Honolulu. He has a BA in the Hawaiian Language from the University of Hawai'i, a BA in Spanish from Rutgers University, and an MLIS from the University of Hawai'i.

About the Illustrator

Storm Kano is a published illustrator of local children's books. Born and raised on O'ahu, she hopes to give back to her community through the art of visual storytelling. When she's not drawing, Storm enjoys exploring the natural beauty of the island and cuddling with her dog, Toby. For more information, visit www.StormKano.art.

ISBN: 978-1-949000-37-5
Library of Congress Control Number: 2024941595

Illustrations by Storm Kano
Design by Jane Gillespie
First Printing, October 2024

BeachHouse Publishing
PO Box 5464 • Kāne'ohe, Hawai'i 96744
info@beachhousepublishing.com
www.beachhousepublishing.com

Printed in China

Follow us on Instagram!

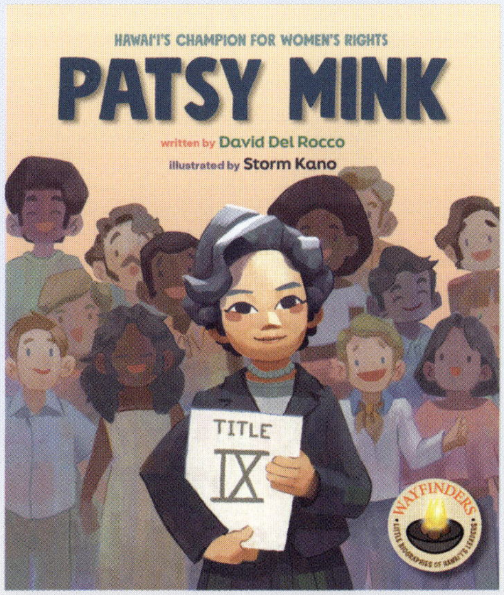

Wayfinders LITTLE BIOGRAPHIES OF HAWAI'I'S LEADERS

WAYFINDERS is a new series of biographies celebrating Hawai'i's leaders—women and men who have helped shape the islands as we know them today. These books shine a light on those well-known and lesser-known educators, scientists, athletes, artists, activists, and political leaders who have transformed Hawai'i and paved the way for future generations.

Patsy Mink, Hawai'i's Champion for Women's Rights is about the mother of Title IX who stood up against racism and sexism and fought for the health and well-being of Hawai'i's women and children, the environment, and gender equality. Maui-born Patsy Mink was a force to be reckoned with and a fierce advocate for Hawai'i's people.

ISBN 978-1-949000-35-1 • 6.625 x 8 inches • 24 pages • $9.95

ʻŌLELO
NOʻEAU